# The Stories In Front Of The Songs

Tim Chaplin

Published by Tim Chaplin, 2024.

While every precaution has been taken in the preparation of this book, the publisher assumes no responsibility for errors or omissions, or for damages resulting from the use of the information contained herein.

THE STORIES IN FRONT OF THE SONGS

**First edition. June 14, 2024.**

Copyright © 2024 Tim Chaplin.

ISBN: 979-8224151165

Written by Tim Chaplin.

# Also by Tim Chaplin

A Mile Away In The Blink Of An Eye
The Stories In Front Of The Songs

Watch for more at https://timchaplin.bandcamp.com.

# Table of Contents

This Road Was Made For The Rain To Run Down/Don't Know Why I Don't Know Why ................ 1

The Truth/Flicker And Die ................ 3

Baby And The Bright Lights/Daisy Chain Fridays ................ 4

The Ring Don't Fit The Same/Boyfriend Gum ................ 5

The Angel Thieves/Silver Rain ................ 6

Endtimes/Go Back To Rosie ................ 7

The River's Name/Taxi Lights ................ 8

Hayley's Hurt My Feelings/Pale Into Insignificance ................ 9

No More Good Days/Some Kinda Saint ................ 10

Sunglasses & Cool Cars/Hit So Hard ................ 11

The Well Of Never Thinking/Red Rocks ................ 12

Tennerman Street/Two Times Means I Am ................ 13

Life Is Like/Blackthorn Lemonade ................ 14

30 Years/No Fast Cargo ................ 15

Who Are The Losers?/Adriana Thing ................ 16

Speed Dive/Molecules ................ 17

Hummingbirds/What Happiness Wants ................ 18

Your Heart And My Mind Will Stay/Beautiful Daisy ................ 19

Found Myself/Festival On Me ................ 20

You Know Where I Live/Time To Go ......................................................... 21

Nobody That You Know/Cobwebs ............................................................. 22

Nothing To Defend/Weird Kissy Thing ...................................................... 23

Green About It/Marilyn Monroe Repeating ............................................. 24

Petal Pushing/Girl Called Crying ................................................................. 25

Lies On/About This Girl ................................................................................ 26

Discography ..................................................................................................... 27

# This Road Was Made For The Rain To Run Down/Don't Know Why I Don't Know Why

---

This was written a little while before starting 'Chrome Plated On Nickel Silver', my first official album. I remember aiming for a Ronettes kinda thing. Springsteen has been detected here too and, looking back, I think I was going for that as well. Bruce himself was massively influenced by the girl group/Spector sound of course. Some of the harmonies on this are very E Street. As with a lot of the album, there are field recordings present. This was often to mask some of the monitor bleed, but not always. There's also some good old backwards guitar - can't argue with that. I think 'peace of heart' was a little phrase I'd written down and finally got to use here. That happens quite a bit, as you shall see.

---

I must have been going for a Jacobites vibe on this one. It's like a mix of two songs from their second LP, 'Robespierre's Velvet Basement'. Check out 'Son Of A French Nobleman' and 'Country Girl'. This remains my favourite album of all time - the best collection of original songs all in one place that isn't a compilation. It was always supposed to be a double album. We'd all have to wait until the nineties for that. The upward key changes are something Dave Kusworth liked to do a lot. Very orgasmic, if I do say so myself. I threw in some twinkly music box/glockenspiel parts. Again, very Danny Federici and Belle and Sebastian. All the songs on 'Chrome Plated' are very layered. This was especially inspired by listening to 'lilac6' by The Lilac Time. It was the first time I'd recorded any actual songs on a computer. I'd previous done some Luminous stuff that way and the software was really only intended for dance music. Short loops and sections to be moved around, rather than full takes of instruments and vocals. I did what I could - often having to split parts into two or three when the software and/or computer ran outta steam. As for plug-ins, I only had a handful to play with. Due to these limitations, I processed every single part independently in another program to give everything more colour, pasted them back in and hoped for the best.

# The Truth/Flicker And Die

I had a song called 'Janglepop' - still do - and this one was kind of like a follow up to that. They were both originally recorded on 4-track with two electric guitar parts. For this version, I wanted acoustic guitars and a very cheap-sounding drum part. The guitars I was never happy with and reversed them to varying degrees on each bar. Each one differently to the other. Someone actually mistook them for a harpsichord - I was happy with that. The wah wah keyboard loop motif was a little nod to 'Genius Of Love' by Tom Tom Club - one my favourite eighties songs and videos.

---

Probably a phrase I stole or misheard from somewhere. Taken from 'Slo-Mo Baby Doll', a reaction to the endless layers of the previous album and recorded on 8-track. I'd been hearing about all the spontaneous Babyshambles demos and fancied a bit of that. I wanted a natural sound for this album. No click track, loops or effects. You can hear a kind of natural drone which is eventually introduced on harmonium part way through. Playing along with what you thought you could hear. Or maybe that was just me. I'd have had it all the way along if the Zip disk was bigger. You can even hear the memory run out before the harmonium has run its course. It's mostly a true story about bumping into an old friend and what he told me. I'd rather have liked it to be a duet, but the lack of vocal partner dictated I sang both parts myself. It was Kusworth's favourite song of mine from this period.

# Baby And The Bright Lights/Daisy Chain Fridays

---

Songs need cool titles. I went through a period of writing songs around the titles. They had to live up to what I deemed to be cool and interesting. This was a little while afterwards, but it's a nice name for a song. Not 'In' but 'And' - very important. Religious imagery in songs is always very powerful. There's a little Johnny Thunders thing in here somewhere too. Oh, and a very big Go-Betweens reference, although I think it was (mostly) subconscious at the time of writing. We're onto the 'For Real In The Real World' album now. I'd been hanging out with Sonic Boom in Rugby, so some of our drinking buddies found their way into the lyrics. The lack of cymbals on most of the album was a Spacemen 3 thing. Dave K was making a pretty rocking album in Leamington at this point, so the overall electric vibe also influenced me. There's a particular kissing gate I have in mind when I get to that line.

---

Sitting on the grass of the school field across the road from where I lived. Probably on a Friday. I came up with the idea when I was in the studio with Nikki Sudden. I was thinking about 'Pleasant Valley Sunday' and thought I might make my own Midlands version of that. The lead guitar part was an afterthought. Often the way with my songs. It came out like 'Somebody Got Murdered', which I'd always loved, but never knew how to play. I found an effect similar to what Mick Jones used live around that time. My little tribute. This song is the first time I really went to town with vocal double tracking and harmonies.

# The Ring Don't Fit The Same/Boyfriend Gum

There's a really great band called Astrid. I saw them play once. One of their songs had a soft but pounding drum part along with the gentle guitars. I didn't know how to do that, so my drums sounded rowdy as fuck. It still somehow worked. Turns out it was probably as simple as using brushes - who knew? For me, this album is very much blue and white - willow pattern. I see sound and music as colours, textures and shapes. Some albums and songs more than others, but this cover really had to be blue and white.

What was I saying about cool titles? This one came from Neighbours. The rest of it is all me. And all her. I wanted harmonica and twangy electric guitar in the breaks, but couldn't decide which should go where. Yep, I used them both on top of each other. A bit clangy, but there ya go. 'The September Sessions' album did originally have another title, but it's now long since forgotten. It was recorded during September, though. A day or two after finishing it, Dave asked me to play in his band. He'd been asking for a while, but this time I unambiguously agreed.

# The Angel Thieves/Silver Rain

It was back to the 8-track for the 'September' album. I was hoping for a La's thing with this song. It originally had a different rhythm, but when it came to recording, I couldn't quite remember it. Still can't, so the shuffle stuck. New Order have been mentioned in comparison, but I can't hear it myself. It's very sentimental. Very bittersweet and childlike. A lot of the words are true. The ones that aren't, still feel like the right ones.

An English August Thursday afternoon. 'How We Used To Live' was named after an old educational programme for schools that I watched as a kid when I was off school ill. Or pretending to be. I wanted this song to be a bit like Kevin Shields's soundtrack to 'Lost In Translation'. A DJ friend and I agreed it ended up more like MBV. There are worse things to sound like. The bulk of it was written in my head as what you hear in the song was actually happening. Not the first time that's happened, as you will very likely find out.

# Endtimes/Go Back To Rosie

This was originally recorded for the 'Slo-Mo' album, but I was never happy with it. You'd be amazed how hard it is to sound like The Velvet Underground. It may all seem rather ramshackle, but you give it a go. Dan Treacy wrote a song about just that. I decided to go for a whole different arrangement this time. The title came from an interview with Coil's John/Jhonn Balance. Pretty sure it was quoted as all one word, although it's often split into two when you see it elsewhere. I like it how it is here. Most of the imagery in the lyrics is real. I had an actual person and place in mind when I wrote it and they are still linked whenever I think about it.

The title is straight from 'Subway Train', the New York Dolls song. I always preferred the version Johnny Thunders did later on 'So Alone'. As usual, the lead guitar part was an afterthought, but it works as a nice hook. The whole song is very Kusworth. Well, at least the melody and vocal. 'I'd Die For You If You Want Me To' is from a Dead Boys song, 'All This And More'.

# The River's Name/Taxi Lights

The title track of this EP was inspired by a film. I just can't remember what it was called and the internet is offering no help. Well, not the right help, at least. It was black and white but recent. Possibly Russian. Definitely co-starring a typewriter. There's a little nod to 'Sailors Of The Highway' by T. Rex, which Nikki once recorded.

I first recorded this for 'Due Style'. That arrangement suited that album, but it was always supposed to be more organic. The sound I was originally thinking about was 'Back In The Crowd' by Tom Waits. The subject is very real, taking place in at least two different cities at different times. The person it's about would very much recognise that if they were ever to hear it.

# Hayley's Hurt My Feelings/Pale Into Insignificance

---

This is one of my most-recorded songs. By which, I mean most recorded by me. The version on 'Derelicting' is the one I'm most happy with. Alliteration is always good in songs and I always knew that. I just didn't know the correct name for it at the time. I don't really write all that many riffs, but this is a pretty cool one I reckon. Very Stones-y all round - in the words and music. I didn't really know anyone called Hayley very well when I wrote this. It wasn't particularly about a specific person, but there was always someone who was like my muse back then. So... maybe. I met Hayley later.

---

Another one of my most-recorded tracks. The version on its very own EP is my favourite. I've felt no need to re-record it since. The twelve-string acoustic guitar really brought it to life. I wrote it with Dave K's 'Paint And Sugar' in mind. A distorted guitar over acoustic guitars. Less than a decade later, I was standing next to Dave playing that very same distorted guitar part.

# No More Good Days/Some Kinda Saint

From an album started on an iPad, with a minimum of overdubs afterwards. The gist of it came from something my friend told me. I stole another part from a book I was reading. The title of the album 'Every Seventh Wave' was something we were talking about as well. You know, how every seventh one is a big one.

A super-layered one, this. Most or all of the guitar parts doubled up too. Started on an iPad, but this album had a whole lot more overdubs on it. That was always the idea. No point making the same thing all over again. This one was called 'Days Either Side'. The song was pretty much all about one person, with a line or two nicked from books. Influence-wise, we're looking at Tom Petty, DK and The Strokes, I'm guessing. Some Psychedelic Furs too. Someone once asked me if it was a Christmas song. I used the word 'saint' more as an example of a perfect person. As in 'enough to make a saint swear' etc. Listening to it now, it sounds huge. If only I could be bothered to lay down so many parts again. Maybe one day...

# Sunglasses & Cool Cars/Hit So Hard

———

I got this title from a chapter in a book about LA punk rock called 'Under the Big Black Sun' by John Doe from X. Lots of rhyming going on in it. Very playful really. Coupla music references in it too. It was from an album called 'Desire Creeps' that was recorded entirely on an iPad. No real instruments or microphones. Just sang straight into the thing. The album gets quite a lot of attention, although it's one of the roughest and weirdest solo ones I've ever done. Funny how this happens quite a bit. I met a girl around this time who told me she was a radar operator. She might have been. Hmm...

———

I wrote this in my head one Christmas Day evening. Was it still Christmas Day if it was evening? Not sure. Anyway, all just written in my head, no guitar or anything. I put it down on paper later. An attempt at a kinda Motown thing. Or northern soul or whatever. There's an acoustic version of it knocking around somewhere as well, but I'm talking about the one on 'Almost Made It Through The Rock 'n' Roll Death Age'. I don't have much more to tell you about the actual song, so let's talk about the album. The classic rock 'n' roll death age is 27, right. I'd already made it - by quite a long way - but I had a few friends who were just hitting it. So there you are.

# The Well Of Never Thinking/Red Rocks

This one always makes me think of Joe Strummer. I know the song I have in my mind now. You probably do too. There's something nice about playing acoustic guitar and singing at the same time. Even nicer if it's all into the same mic or - better still - no mic at all. 'Fire Escapism' was an album of songs with medium-sized arrangements punctuated by little lo-fi acoustic ditties. Yep, this was one of the acoustic ones.

We all know the iconic Colorado amphitheatre, don't we? They're two nice words that go together well. The bit about 'carrying some disease' kinda predicted Covid. By the time the album was out, so was it. That happens quite a bit in songs. They may not make perfect sense at the time, or even any sense whatsoever. As long as they feel right, that's the main thing. They might tell you something you didn't know. Quite possibly about yourself. Quite possibly years later. That little phrase you sing as you work up a song, never intending to actually keep it - yep, that's probably gonna be the title you'd better get used to.

# Tennerman Street/Two Times Means I Am

This isn't a real place, but the place I see in my mind's eye whenever I hear or think about it is. It's mostly fantasy writing, except that at the playgroup my aunty helped run, kids had glue spreaders that more often than not ended up in mugs of coffee instead of water. Easily done.

We're still on the 'Nowhere To Fall Down From' album. Well, just about. You know that superstitious/OCD thing - if I do/don't step on this crack, next door's dog will die? It's sort of like that. Or she loves me, she loves me not. Romantic pop songs are great. I've done a few.

# Life Is Like/Blackthorn Lemonade

---

The title track to a very red album. At least the cover is. It was supposed to be a follow-up to 'Desire Creeps', but instead of being entirely made on an iPad with no extra equipment, it was made on a Mac. I expected the singing to sound quite rough, but it turned out pretty well. I've done most of my vocals that way ever since. I saw a photo of Jason Pierce recording at home and there was a sign that read, 'My Life Is Like A Shangri-Las Song'. That was the starting point. You may know a few of the six people referenced in the lyrics. If not, lucky you - you get to have your first time right now. I will provide you with a little clue, though - the Arnold isn't Arnie.

---

This one was inspired by a film I can remember properly. Well, with a little help from some people's favourite search engine. It's called 'The Love Witch'. This song has a bit of a Baroque thing going on with the harpsichord part. Not much more to tell you, except check out The Left Banke if you haven't already. Blackthorn lemonade probably isn't even a real drink. Maybe it could be - who's brave enough to make it?

# 30 Years/No Fast Cargo

---

These past two songs come from the 'Eighties' album. '30 Years' is a drone-based number. Sort of Telescopes/Spacemen 3/Spiritualized-esque. The Joneses mentioned are of the Dylan, Pixies and Supremes varieties. Go get 'em...

---

This was a stab at the very early Bowie period. Well, one of the many early periods. Probably one of the first times I used an electric twelve-string guitar. Pounding, jangling mod, at least to my ears. That said, I'm currently wearing an ear-obstructing trapper hat, so maybe don't take my word for it.

# Who Are The Losers?/Adriana Thing

These tracks are from 'Mega City Dreaming'. I suppose a nod to the band and Camden comic shop. If I'm gonna do any chugging rock stuff, I make sure it has a bit of a melancholy edge to it. That or just some general weirdness. I have indeed had lunch in a cafe of clocks.

This is like a cousin of the previous song. Or a sister. I remember recording the vocals for it early one autumn evening. Another melancholy chugger. Lots of guitar layers going on, by the sounds of it. It's not easy pretending to be different people when you only have one pair of hands and are too lazy to even change instruments.

# Speed Dive/Molecules

Very Ian Hunter/Mott The Hoople. I remember thinking that even as I was writing and recording it. We're onto the 'Sank You' album at this point. Lots of lyrics here. Much more than I'd usually do. It's a long track for me too. One of those songs that seemed as though it really should be about someone. I know who that person is now.

---

This came to me in a dream. Lots of songs do, but I'm not usually able to remember them like I did with this one. College rock if you're from the Midlands as opposed to Minnesota, say. I remember trying to emphasise the noisy Dinosaur Jr. section. Some weird chords in the gaps as well. Please don't ask me what they're called.

# Hummingbirds/What Happiness Wants

This is really sad. At least to me. I can feel it hurting, even now. Several girls all mixed up into one song. I just counted five. Some even coming back for more. Fuck.

If Bruce Springsteen came from Warwickshire... Or something. Or summat. Works nicely as the closing number on 'Sank You'. Yeah, I know, my stories are getting shorter today, but I'm very wary of rambling and spelling things out that might be fun for you to look into yourself.

# Your Heart And My Mind Will Stay/ Beautiful Daisy

---

Here we go with 'Your Fireworks Or Mine?'. Is it me or is this BJM doing Slade unplugged? Yep, just me. In my dreams. I really don't know how I managed to record this many songs. Writing them isn't so bad, but recording - at least for me - is pretty tedious. It was a very productive period. I always felt - particularly around this time - that I needed to hurry up.

---

BJM again. How d'ya even play slide guitar? I know you know that I don't know. A little girl, playing in the garden, not far from a major military garrison. Something lands in the soil next to her. Close one.

# Found Myself/Festival On Me

I have this recurring dream where I find myself on top of a steep wall or roof and the only way down is to jump. It's pretty high up. Much more so than I'd really like. I promise myself this will be the last time I do this. Until the next dream. I'm sure someone can tell me what this all means. I suspect I kinda already know.

'Screaming Blue Murder' is one of my acoustic albums. Sounds like I might be using my bronze resonator guitar on this. The title comes from something a friend told me upon her return from a local shindig. I loved it and knew I'd use it somewhere eventually. Thanks, E.

# You Know Where I Live/Time To Go

You can either end an album with a sad song or a happy one. Well, there are other alternatives, but it's often what I do. This is happy-ish. At the very least, you could call it playful. Listen for the sound of my clock on the fade. Bloody thing. It's still right here behind me now. I'll never learn.

I recorded a bunch of songs that I wasn't much fancying turning into an album. I'd just done a few of those with fairly lengthy tracklistings and quite liked the idea of a change. Four EPs it was. This reminds me of one of The Wildhearts' later songs. I just found which one. Can you? Bit of Kusworth and Perrett going on here too. As usual.

# Nobody That You Know/Cobwebs

---

I wrote this thinking of a very specific place. Cool starting a song with 'Hi', right? C'mon, I thought so. It starts off in one town, but the manikin is in another. Pigeon Street and The Doors are also here, for some reason. You can be like no one the person who's telling you that knows. That could be good or bad. Or both.

---

If bad things have happened - even if they've happened over and over and over, for years and years and years - they don't have to happen again. I know what most of this song is about. A few bits might reveal themselves to me later. It's usually the way with these things.

# Nothing To Defend/Weird Kissy Thing

There was a book in our middle school library called 'High Treason at Catfish Bend'. We always found the title very funny for some reason. I suppose it is, on the right day. Nikki Sudden did a song called 'Pirate Girls' with a list of real women in it. I fancied a go at that. Luckily, all of the initials rhymed.

We're at the end of the EPs now. Robyn Hitchcock and Andy Partridge made an EP called 'Planet England'. I'm referencing their song 'Turn Me On, Deadman'. They're referencing The Beatles. I used to see that bootleg around. Bit of electric twelve-string again here. My lyrics had got stranger and more surreal by this point. We can probably blame Andy and R. Pollard.

# Green About It/Marilyn Monroe Repeating

---

We're almost up-to-date here. I did another acoustic album. It was called 'Plague Of Rocks'. I think I got the title from Sally Bayley, a modern literary giant. In my opinion, someone who has reconfigured what writing can be. The places in this song had to be alliterative, but they are very real. All the opposites were me challenging myself to find enough words in the manner of 'Hello, Goodbye'.

---

Who would put James Dean Bradfield, Andy Warhol and Fred West into a pop song? Who would even want to? I think this title came from a book by Gordon Burn. Or at least the idea of it did. Anyway, it's not 'Candle In The Wind'. Nasty subject, pretty sound. At least on the last verse.

# Petal Pushing/Girl Called Crying

Here we go with the 'Thinking In English' album. This song probably has the weirdest lyrics I've ever written. They come from the titles of books on my shelves, so they partly wrote themselves. The second part, maybe not so much, but certainly the main verse came from books. I wonder if you can spot or guess any of them...

I'm thinking about Robert Pollard whenever I encounter this song. Particularly the album with Tommy Keene as Keene Brothers. There's very likely a bit of XTC going on here as well. Vaguely avant garde lyrics. One of my favourites on this album.

# Lies On/About This Girl

---

I loved the Lil Peep documentary 'Everybody's Everything' and listened to his music quite a lot around that time. This song is very much informed by that, although you probably wouldn't notice and still might not do now. The other main source is 'The First Cut Is The Deepest'. That's probably much more apparent. I wasn't sure it quite fitted in with the rest of the album, but I've come around to it now.

---

Okay, we're on the last song. Remember earlier I told you that I tend to finish albums with a (fairly obviously) sad or happy song? Well, you can probably guess which one this is. I think I wrote all or most of it in my head while watching a film. Pretty sure I know which one, but I won't name it in case I'm mistaken. I had someone in mind as well, but the film helped birth the whole thing. This is the first of a series of songs on a very particular subject. I sent them all out into the world via various outlets. It was the least I could do.

# Discography

**C.D. E.P. self-released pro CD-R 1998**

1. Janglepop

2. The Same

3. Sudden Burst Of Nothing

4. Sophie Sometimes

**Cassette compilation with Shadders? On Me Lungs? fanzine volume 3 issue 1 1999**

1. Janglepop

**Beware Of The Ricochet Volume 2 cassette compilation album on Best Kept Secret (LIE 017) 2000**

1. Janglepop

**Here Comes Down 7" single on Plastic Pancake (Plastic Pancake 13) 2000**

A1. Here Comes Down

B1. Better Yesterday?

B2. Shine Out

**Bliss Volume Eighty Seven cassette compilation album on Bliss (Bliss 087) 2000**

1. Janglepop

2. Sophie Sometimes

**The 22nd Floor cassette album on Best Kept Secret (LIE 037) 2001**

A1. Hayley's Hurt My Feelings

A2. Walk In The Sun

A3. What Do I Do?

A4. See You On The Other Side

A5. Sophie Sometimes

B1. Not What I Was

B2. That Someone's Not You

B3. All I Do Is Write It Down

B4. Empty Blues

B5. Back 2 U

**We are not alone - songs for the lo-fi generation - volume six cassette compilation album on Best Kept Secret (LIE 043) 2002**

1. Pale Into Insignificance

**Chrome Plated On Nickel Silver CD album on Tara Records (TARA 001) 2005**

1. Everybody In Here Loves You

2. Crash-Land

3. Try

4. Space In Time

5. The Truth

6. Accept Or Deny

7. This Road Was Made For The Rain To Run Down

8. Jemma With A J

9. Don't Know Why I Don't Know Why

10. Seems Like Sinking

**Download from timchaplin.com 2005**

1. Don't Know Why I Don't Know Why

**Chrome Plated On Nickel Silver download album on Tara Records (TARA 001) 2006**

1. Everybody In Here Loves You

2. Crash-Land

3. Try

4. Space In Time

5. The Truth

6. Accept Or Deny

7. This Road Was Made For The Rain To Run Down

8. Jemma With A J

9. Don't Know Why I Don't Know Why

10. Seems Like Sinking

**Exclusive download from myspace.com/timchaplinluminous 2007**

1. Let's All Make Friends

**I Would Write A Thousand Words Television Personalities tribute CD/CD-R compilation album on The Beautiful Music (BEAUTY 015) 2007**

1. Stop And Smell The Roses

**Slo-Mo Baby Doll CD album on Golden Pathway (GPV030) 2007**

1. Don't Take It To Heart

2. Close To Home

3. Drift

4. Suspended

5. Sarah Jane's

6. Endtimes

7. Believe You Me

8. Flicker And Die

9. Alonely

10. Disowned

**Slo-Mo Baby Doll promo CD album - as above, but in plastic wallet with different inserts - on Golden Pathway (GPV030) 2007**

1. Don't Take It To Heart

2. Close To Home

3. Drift

4. Suspended

5. Sarah Jane's

6. Endtimes

7. Believe You Me

8. Flicker And Die

9. Alonely

10. Disowned

**The Watercolour Lane EP download on 23 seconds (sec.009) 2007**

1. Watercolour Lane

2. The Man Who Made The Key

3. The Stars Fell On Sally Brown

4. Lost Cause

**The '80's Girls EP download on 23 seconds (sec.014) 2008**

1. Silver Mac

2. They Don't Know

3. Only You

4. It Must Have Been Love

**For Real In The Real World download album on Tara Records (TARA 005) 2008**

1. Hour Glass

2. How Long 'Til I Let Go?

3. Setting It Straight

4. The Ring Don't Fit The Same

5. Alive, Actually?

6. Daisy Chain Fridays

7. Catholic Hill

8. Baby And the Bright Lights

9. Angeline

10. Used To Your Eyes

**The September Sessions download album on Tara Records (TARA 006) 2008**

1. Candy Apple Grey

2. Some Gurl

3. Because Of You

4. Sparkle

5. Boyfriend Gum

6. Hazel Eyes

7. The Angel Thieves

8. Like Tarka Did

9. Ivy League

10. Rainy Blue

11. Runaround

12. Closing Time

**23 Evergreens download compilation album on 23 seconds (sec.023) 2008**

1. They Don't Know

**Series Two Compilation Vol. 18 CD-R album on Series Two Records (#46) 2009**

1. Pretty

**Series Two Retrospective Compilation # 4 CD-R album on Series Two Records (#93) 2010**

1. Broken By The Years

**Gone Wrong Days download album on Corporate Records 2010**

1. The Fine Line

2. Forever Understand

3. Tuesday Trilogy

4. Good As Gold

5. Take Away

6. Broken By The Years

7. One More Boy Called Trouble

8. Boys Who'll Give Her Everything

9. 2am

10. Flying

**Fusion Compilation 5ummer download album on Fusion (FN_16) 2010**

1. The Angel Thieves

**How We Used To Live download album on Corporate Records 2010**

1. Sunday Dates

2. Baby Love

3. Crybaby (Again)

4. Silver Rain

5. Rock-A-Bye Baby

6. Nowhere For A While

7. Dim Stars

8. Hayley Jane

9. Sweet To Say

10. Ten Minutes More

**Honesty download album on Tara Records/ timchaplin.bandcamp.com (TARA 011) 2011**

1. Baby

2. Baby Blue Sky

3. Our Lady Of The Roses

4. Teenage Love Anxiety

5. Walk In The Sun

6. So She Says

7. Q & A

8. Princess Diaries

9. Your Top Ten

10. Sophie Sometimes

11. Someone I Used To Know

12. With Cracks

**Due Style download album on Tara Records/ timchaplin.bandcamp.com (TARA 017) 2012**

1. Clarity

2. Slow Beach

3. Miss Black America

4. Churched

5. Taxi Lights

6. Due Style

**Daisy Chain Fridays cassette/download EP on Bleeding Gold Records (BG022) 2012**

1. Daisy Chain Fridays

2. Hazel Eyes

3. The Answer In Your Eyes

4. Disowned

5. This One

**TC-BG 1 download mix from soundcloud.com/bleedinggold 2012**

1. Right Is Wrong (Warped & Whipped) - Tim Chaplin

2. Used Cars - Bruce Springsteen

3. Somebody Got Murdered - The Clash

4. Oh, My (Stripped Down Mix) - Factory Kids

5. I Wish I Never Saw The Sunshine - The Ronettes

6. Country Girl - Jacobites

7. Glowworm - The Apples In Stereo

8. Come Pick Me Up - Ryan Adams

9. The Boy Done Wrong Again - Belle And Sebastian

10. She's The Only One (Scratched & Inhaled) - Tim Chaplin

11. The Light That Failed - Atlas Sound

12. The Whisper Of Your Mind - The Lilac Time

**TC-BG 1 download mix from soundcloud.com/bleedinggold 2012**

1. Right Is Wrong (Warped & Whipped)

2. She's The Only One (Scratched & Inhaled)

**11"x14" BGR POSTER with download on Bleeding Gold Records (BG024) 2012**

1. Dizzy

**Broken So Bad download album on Bleeding Gold Records (BG037) 2012**

1. The Truth

2. This Road Was Made For The Rain To Run Down

3. Let's All Make Friends

4. Jemma With A J

5. Don't Know Why I Don't Know Why

6. Disowned

7. Sarah Jane's

8. Flicker And Die

9. Daisy Chain Fridays

10. Angeline

11. Baby And The Bright Lights

12. Watercolour Lane

13. Boyfriend Gum

14. The Angel Thieves

15. Broken By The Years

16. Good As Gold

17. Flying

18. Silver Rain

19. Dim Stars

20. Rock-A-Bye Baby

**Broken So Bad vinyl LP on Bleeding Gold Records (BG037) 2012**

A1. The Truth

A2. Jemma With A J

A3. Sarah Jane's

A4. Flicker And Die

A5. Daisy Chain Fridays

B1. Boyfriend Gum

B2. The Angel Thieves

B3. Good As Gold

B4. Dim Stars

B5. Rock-A-Bye Baby

**I'd Die For You If You Want Me To download mini album on Tara Records/timchaplin.bandcamp.com (TARA 021) 2014**

1. Ladies In Waiting

2. Month Of Sundays

3. Almost Grown

4. Endtimes

5. Same Rain

6. What Do I Do?

7. Go Back To Rosie

8. This One

**The River's Name EP download on Tara Records/ timchaplin.bandcamp.com (TARA 024) 2014**

1. Zlatina Ballerina

2. Song To Myself

3. Sorry Somehow

4. Shame

5. The River's Name

**Glazed/Touch A Nerve? download single on Tara Records/ timchaplin.bandcamp.com (TARA 026) 2015**

1. Glazed

2. Touch A Nerve?

**Aw, Man/21 download single on Tara Records/ timchaplin.bandcamp.com (TARA 027) 2015**

1. Aw, Man

2. 21

**Sally's Arms/Morning, Marie download single on Tara Records/ timchaplin.bandcamp.com (TARA 028) 2015**

1. Sally's Arms

2. Morning, Marie

**Boy To Make Me Worry download album on Bleeding Gold Records (BG101) 2016**

1. All The Way From Nowhere

2. Love You To The Moon And Back Again

3. Alone

4. Stratospheric

5. Fine

6. No Wonder

7. Uncle Ron's Theme

8. So She Says

9. So She Says (Instrumental Mix)

10. Fortune Cookies

11. Fortune Cookies (Instrumental Mix)

12. Shot Down

13. Shot Down (Anti Guitar Mix)

14. Shot Down (Stripped Down Mix)

15. And So It Goes

16. And So It Goes (Stripped Down Mix)

17. Wrong

18. The Last Thing

19. Stay Away

20. She Said

21. The Answer In Your Eyes

22. Cotton Wool

23. Gonna Get To You

24. Fade Away

25. On Your Own

26. A Picture Of You

27. Angels

28. Same Bus Home

29. Hazel Eyes

30. Anthology

31. Rag Tag Girl

32. Wrong Way Out

33. Damage

34. Always, Always, Always

35. 11:17

36. Last Train

37. Antiquity

38. Black And Blue

39. Secret Place

**Boy To Make Me Worry double vinyl LP on Bleeding Gold Records (BG101) 2016**

A1. Stratospheric

A2. Fine

A3. No Wonder

A4. So She Says

A5. Shot Down

A6. And So It Goes

B1. Wrong

B2. The Last Thing

B3. Stay Away

B4. She Said

B5. The Answer In Your Eyes

C1. Cotton Wool

C2. Fade Away

C3. On Your Own

D1. A Picture Of You

D2. Hazel Eyes

D3. Rag Tag Girl

D4. Damage

D5. 11:17

D6. Antiquity

**Girl To Make You Happy streamed mix on soundcloud.com/bleedinggold 2016**

1. Sweet Unknown - Cranes

2. She May Call You Up Tonight - The Left Banke

3. Carolay - Crazy Horse

4. Five One Zero Lovers - Lazycame

5. Church Of Wilson (4-Track) - Cotton Mather

6. Guest Informant - The Fall

7. Red Cadillac And A Black Moustache - Warren Smith

8. Needles And Pins - Jackie DeShannon

9. With A Cantaloupe Girlfriend - The Three O'Clock

10. Out Of My Mind - Buffalo Springfield

11. AAA - Paul Westerberg

**Taxi Lights download EP on Tara Records/timchaplin.bandcamp.com (TARA 034) 2016**

1. Taxi Lights

2. Passed The Test, Lost Your Mind

3. Creeping, Crawling

4. Acid Breakdown

**Derelicting download album on Tara Records/timchaplin.bandcamp.com (TARA 035) 2016**

1. Black Star Liner

2. Take What You Want From Me

3. 1989

4. Dumb

5. Goosebumps

6. Absolutely You

7. Neck On The Line

8. Only Jo

9. Animals

10. Your Oblivion

11. Hayley's Hurt My Feelings

12. Pop Quiz

**Pale Into Insignificance download EP on Tara Records/ timchaplin.bandcamp.com (TARA 036) 2016**

1. Pale Into Insignificance

2. Shanna

3. Whatsoever

4. Winning Easier

**Burgundy Blues download EP on Tara Records/ timchaplin.bandcamp.com (TARA 042) 2017**

1. Arena Says

2. Beat Police

3. Burgundy Blues

4. Once In A While

5. No Solution

**Every Seventh Wave download album on Tara Records/ timchaplin.bandcamp.com (TARA 043) 2017**

1. In Restless Years

2. Lost In Translation

3. No More Good Days

4. Onwards & Upwards

5. Happening

6. Cahoots

7. Codename: Oblivious

8. Hated

9. Dismissing Miss Material

10. You Can't Break A Broken Dream

**Just Wow download EP on Tara Records/ timchaplin.bandcamp.com (TARA 048) 2017**

1. From There To Somewhere

2. Dude

3. Little Boy Left

4. Just Wow

**Days Either Side download album on Tara Records/ timchaplin.bandcamp.com (TARA 049) 2017**

1. Future Architect

2. Some Kinda Saint

3. Alina

4. Ain't No Daddy

5. Gram Rock

6. Midweek

7. Baby So Bored

8. Nessa Sara Lee

9. Sweet As

**Desire Creeps digital album 2018**

1. Blood On My Hands

2. Drug Power Lust

3. Falling To The Floor

4. Lover Liar Lover

5. Milly Molly Mandy

6. Desire Creeps

7. Natural Blue

8. Wanted Anyone

9. Sunglasses & Cool Cars

10. Fireman Phase

**Different Currents digital EP 2019**

1. Ah

2. Repo Man

3. Different Currents

4. You're The Only Thing I Do

5. White Zombie

**An Taobh Tuathail on RTE RnaG - third of three special twentieth anniversary shows of exclusive music 2.5.19**

1. 666

**Summer 2019 streamed playlist on Tim Chaplin Spotify profile 2019**

1. Bird Of The World - Bill Fox

2. The Mercury Girl - The Cleaners From Venus

3. California Girls - The Magnetic Fields

4. Rose, 1956 - Waxahatchee

5. When You Walk In The Room - Jackie DeShannon

6. Girls Of Wild Strawberries - Guided By Voices

7. Jennifer Save Me - Golden Smog

8. Everyone You Meet - The Clientele

9. Silver Mac - Westworld

10. Ma Blond Est Partie - Amadie Breaux, Ophey Breaux, Cleoma Breaux

11. Real True Lover - Marc Jonson

12. Lovely Life To Leave - Alex Dingley

13. No Substitute - Rachel Goswell

14. Coma Girl - Joe Strummer & The Mescaleros

15. Divvy Cabs - Picturebox

16. Death And The Maiden - The Verlaines

17. Island Of Lost Lucys - Keene Brothers

18. Dylan Thomas - Better Oblivion Community Centre

19. Druglife - East River Pipe

20. Little Rage - The Mice

## Almost Made It Through The Rock 'n' Roll Death Age digital album 2019

1. Melia Jackson

2. Hit So Hard

3. Crying Crossing Roads

4. Rock 'n' Roll Death Age

5. Jennifer Lazy

6. Let Me Go Too Tight

7. Judge-Me-Mental

8. Mad Sad Fad

9. Henrietta

10. Radar Operator

11. Nite, Lovey, I Love Ya

12. Stickin' To Me

13. Tucson

**Chrome Plated On Nickel Silver download album reissue on timchaplin.bandcamp.com 2019**

1. Everybody In Here Loves You

2. Crash-Land

3. Try

4. Space In Time

5. The Truth

6. Accept Or Deny

7. This Road Was Made For The Rain To Run Down

8. Jemma With A J

9. Don't Know Why I Don't Know Why

10. Seems Like Sinking

**Slo-Mo Baby Doll download album reissue on timchaplin.bandcamp.com 2019**

1. Don't Take It To Heart

2. Close To Home

3. Drift

4. Suspended

5. Sarah Jane's

6. Endtimes

7. Believe You Me

8. Flicker And Die

9. Alonely

10. Disowned

**For Real In The Real World download album reissue on timchaplin.bandcamp.com 2019**

1. Hour Glass

2. How Long 'Til I Let Go?

3. Setting It Straight

4. The Ring Don't Fit The Same

5. Alive, Actually?

6. Daisy Chain Fridays

7. Catholic Hill

8. Baby And the Bright Lights

9. Angeline

10. Used To Your Eyes

# THE STORIES IN FRONT OF THE SONGS

**The September Sessions download album reissue on timchaplin.bandcamp.com 2019**

1. Candy Apple Grey

2. Some Gurl

3. Because Of You

4. Sparkle

5. Boyfriend Gum

6. Hazel Eyes

7. The Angel Thieves

8. Like Tarka Did

9. Ivy League

10. Rainy Blue

11. Runaround

12. Closing Time

**Gone Wrong Days download album reissue on timchaplin.bandcamp.com 2019**

1. The Fine Line

2. Forever Understand

3. Tuesday Trilogy

4. Good As Gold

5. Take Away

6. Broken By The Years

7. One More Boy Called Trouble

8. Boys Who'll Give Her Everything

9. 2am

10. Flying

**How We Used To Live download album reissue on timchaplin.bandcamp.com 2019**

1. Sunday Dates

2. Baby Love

3. Crybaby (Again)

4. Silver Rain

5. Rock-A-Bye Baby

6. Nowhere For A While

7. Dim Stars

8. Hayley Jane

9. Sweet To Say

10. Ten Minutes More

**Fire Escapism digital album 2020**

1. Black Heart

2. TTG

3. Truth Train

4. Witch Are You?

5. The Well Of Never Thinking

6. I Fought The Sun

7. I Can't See For Shame

8. Born On Wednesday

9. Elodie

10. Over Ran Over

11. Dead

12. Subfriction

13. My Machine

14. Seems Like Me

15. Bad At All

16. Sheepskin Drum

17. Witch?

18. Funny Mirrors

19. Tell Me When

20. Ba-Da Da-Da

**Honey, Like I Do digital album 2020**

1. This Road Was Made For The Rain To Run Down

2. Don't Know Why I Don't Know Why

3. Jemma With A J

4. The Truth

5. Disowned

6. Flicker And Die

7. Sarah Jane's

8. Baby And The Bright Lights

9. Setting It Straight

10. Angeline

11. Daisy Chain Fridays

12. How Long 'Til I Let Go?

13. The Ring Don't Fit The Same

14. Because Of You

15. Boyfriend Gum

16. The Angel Thieves

17. Broken By The Years

18. Good As Gold

19. Silver Rain

20. Dim Stars

**Reverse Autumn digital album 2020**

1. Oh-So Over Me

2. Obliterated Dreams

3. So Many Signs

4. Rapunzel, Rapunzel

5. Pretty Vows

6. Overboard

7. Oh, Little

8. Maybe March And May

9. Love Resembling

10. Graceless

11. Emily & He

12. Fading Faces

13. Destiny, Man

14. Cry Baby no. 17

15. Slowly, Cat

16. Pretty All Day

**Reverse Autumn: Influences & Inspirations streamed playlist on Tim Chaplin Spotify profile 2020**

1. Obliterated Dreams - Tim Chaplin

2. Baby Learns To Crawl - Paul Westerberg

3. Lily, Rosemary And The Jack Of Hearts - Bob Dylan

4. Slowly, Cat - Tim Chaplin

5. Jesamine - The Casuals

6. Birdshead - Robyn Hitchcock

7. Cry Baby no. 17 - Tim Chaplin

8. Hellhole Ratrace - Girls

9. Hold That Thought - The Brian Jonestown Massacre

10. Pretty Vows - Tim Chaplin

**Honey, Like I Do, Too digital album 2020**

1. Endtimes

2. Go Back To Rosie

3. Song To Myself

4. Sorry Somehow

5. The River's Name

6. Sally's Arms

7. Taxi Lights

8. Goosebumps

9. Take What You Want From Me

10. Only Jo

11. Hayley's Hurt My Feelings

12. Shanna

13. Pale Into Insignificance

14. Beat Police

15. No More Good Days

16. Lost In Translation

17. Hated

18. Just Wow

19. Baby So Bored

20. Some Kinda Saint

**Nowhere To Fall Down From digital album 2020**

1. Red Rocks

2. Total TV

3. Black Reality

4. Rocky, Rock The Boat

5. Tennerman Street

6. Lo-ove

7. Du Mi O Dae

8. Cruel 2 B Kind 2 yr X

9. In These Moments

10. Hellfire

11. Stitches

12. Sicka Joking

13. Evil Eye

14. Two Times Means I Am

**Desire Creeps download album reissue on timchaplin.bandcamp.com 2020**

1. Blood On My Hands

2. Drug Power Lust

3. Falling To The Floor

4. Lover Liar Lover

5. Milly Molly Mandy

6. Desire Creeps

7. Natural Blue

8. Wanted Anyone

9. Sunglasses & Cool Cars

10. Fireman Phase

**Different Currents download EP reissue on timchaplin.bandcamp.com 2020**

1. Ah

2. Repo Man

3. Different Currents

4. You're The Only Thing I Do

5. White Zombie

**Almost Made It Through The Rock 'n' Roll Death Age download album reissue on timchaplin.bandcamp.com 2020**

1. Melia Jackson

2. Hit So Hard

3. Crying Crossing Roads

4. Rock 'n' Roll Death Age

5. Jennifer Lazy

6. Let Me Go Too Tight

7. Judge-Me-Mental

8. Mad Sad Fad

9. Henrietta

10. Radar Operator

11. Nite, Lovey, I Love Ya

12. Stickin' To Me

13. Tucson

**Fire Escapism download album reissue on timchaplin.bandcamp.com 2020**

1. Black Heart

2. TTG

3. Truth Train

4. Witch Are You?

5. The Well Of Never Thinking

6. I Fought The Sun

7. I Can't See For Shame

8. Born On Wednesday

9. Elodie

10. Over Ran Over

11. Dead

12. Subfriction

13. My Machine

14. Seems Like Me

15. Bad At All

16. Sheepskin Drum

17. Witch?

18. Funny Mirrors

19. Tell Me When

20. Ba-Da Da-Da

**Honey, Like I Do download album reissue on timchaplin.bandcamp.com 2020**

1. This Road Was Made For The Rain To Run Down

2. Don't Know Why I Don't Know Why

3. Jemma With A J

4. The Truth

5. Disowned

6. Flicker And Die

7. Sarah Jane's

8. Baby And The Bright Lights

9. Setting It Straight

10. Angeline

11. Daisy Chain Fridays

12. How Long 'Til I Let Go?

13. The Ring Don't Fit The Same

14. Because Of You

15. Boyfriend Gum

16. The Angel Thieves

17. Broken By The Years

18. Good As Gold

19. Silver Rain

20. Dim Stars

**Reverse Autumn download album reissue on timchaplin.bandcamp.com 2020**

1. Oh-So Over Me

2. Obliterated Dreams

3. So Many Signs

4. Rapunzel, Rapunzel

5. Pretty Vows

6. Overboard

7. Oh, Little

8. Maybe March And May

9. Love Resembling

10. Graceless

11. Emily & He

12. Fading Faces

13. Destiny, Man

14. Cry Baby no. 17

15. Slowly, Cat

16. Pretty All Day

**Honey, Like I Do, Too download album reissue on timchaplin.bandcamp.com 2020**

1. Endtimes

2. Go Back To Rosie

3. Song To Myself

4. Sorry Somehow

5. The River's Name

6. Sally's Arms

7. Taxi Lights

8. Goosebumps

9. Take What You Want From Me

10. Only Jo

11. Hayley's Hurt My Feelings

12. Shanna

13. Pale Into Insignificance

14. Beat Police

15. No More Good Days

16. Lost In Translation

17. Hated

18. Just Wow

19. Baby So Bored

20. Some Kinda Saint

**Nowhere To Fall Down From download album reissue on timchaplin.bandcamp.com 2020**

1. Red Rocks

2. Total TV

3. Black Reality

4. Rocky, Rock The Boat

5. Tennerman Street

6. Lo-ove

7. Du Mi O Dae

8. Cruel 2 B Kind 2 yr X

9. In These Moments

10. Hellfire

11. Stitches

12. Sicka Joking

13. Evil Eye

14. Two Times Means I Am

**Life Is Like download album on timchaplin.bandcamp.com and digital 2021**

1. Life Is Like

2. Ali Allegorically

3. 1999

4. Inside The Moon

5. Daddy's Eyes

6. Don't Believe In Ghosts

7. growingupslowandidontknow

8. There's A Hole

9. Pack It Up

10. Mic Tie Sunshine

11. Skin & Bone

12. Still My Sun

13. Underwater

**Like No Other download album on timchaplin.bandcamp.com and digital 2021**

1. Had It With You

2. Sad Magic

3. Alright Girl

4. All The Pictures Of Me Are Covered In You

5. Wednesday Lover

6. Separate Ways

7. Muddle My Mind

8. Death In The Rain

9. Wild Heather

10. Since Ginny Jumped In

11. She Comes To Me In Debt

12. Ghost Train

13. Like No Other

**Pockets Of Rain download album on timchaplin.bandcamp.com and digital 2021**

1. The Rash

2. Constant Wrong

3. Envy Green

4. No Names

5. Four And Twenty Hands

6. Solo Flight

7. I'm Not Trying To Not Tell You

8. Kite On A Hill

9. Postcards To And From Spain (Valencia)

10. So Not The One

11. Why Don't You Watutsi

12. Touch Love

13. Looks Like High To The Untrained Eye

14. Millionaire

15. Witness Man

**Pockets Of Rain: Influences & Inspirations streamed playlist on Tim Chaplin Spotify profile 2021**

1. Looks Like High To The Untrained Eye - Tim Chaplin

2. Come Dancing - The Kinks

3. Corner Shops - DRINKS

4. Millionaire - Tim Chaplin

5. Come With Me - Dave Kusworth & The Tenderhooks

6. Say You Miss Me - 2017 Remaster - Wilco

7. Four And Twenty Hands - Tim Chaplin

8. Standing In Line - Astrid

9. I Am A Tree - Guided By Voices

10. Postcards To And From Spain (Valencia) - Tim Chaplin

**18-21 streamed playlist on Tim Chaplin Spotify profile 2022**

1. Milly Molly Mandy

2. Desire Creeps

3. Fireman Phase

4. You're The Only Thing I Do

5. Stickin' To Me

6. Hit So Hard

7. Tell Me When

8. Funny Mirrors

9. Oh, Little

10. Obliterated Dreams

11. Tennerman Street

12. Two Times Means I Am

13. Red Rocks

14. Underwater

15. Still My Sun

16. Since Ginny Jumped In

17. Death In The Rain

18. Like No Other

19. Postcards To And From Spain (Valencia)

20. Four And Twenty Hands

21. Looks Like High To The Untrained Eye

**Packets Of Oblivion download EP on timchaplin.bandcamp.com and digital 2022**

1. S.A.D.

2. Meaner Now

3. Vampire Weeks

4. Packets Of Oblivion

**Eighties download album on timchaplin.bandcamp.com and digital 2022**

1. Shone Madly Upon

2. Este

3. Blackthorn Lemonade

4. Disconnection

5. You Let The Lexicon

6. Holes In My Memory

7. Noonday Demon

8. Wrong So Wrong

9. 30 Years

10. No Plain Sailing

**Mega City Dreaming download album on timchaplin.bandcamp.com and digital 2022**

1. Something Wrong With Something

2. No Fast Cargo

3. Catch You Can

4. Dew 2 Blue Eyes

5. Remnants

6. Camera Camera

7. Who Are The Losers?

8. Picking Holes In God

9. Yer Whites

10. So Long

11. Cope With

12. The Day That Never Came

13. I Won Some

14. Open Your Heart

15. Happiness Gun

16. Red To Red To Green

17. Adriana Thing

18. Everything Is Anything You Want

19. Mega City Dreaming

**Mega City Dreaming: Influences & Inspirations streamed playlist on Tim Chaplin Spotify profile 2022**

1. Who Are The Losers? - Tim Chaplin

2. I Wanna Be Free - The Lizards/Epic Soundtracks

3. Silent Film Star - Paul Westerberg

4. Dew 2 Blue Eyes - Tim Chaplin

5. A Hermes Blues - White Fence

6. The Book Of Love - The Magnetic Fields

7. No Fast Cargo - Tim Chaplin

8. You've Got A Habit Of Leaving - 2014 Remaster - Davy Jones (And The Lower Third)

9. Andnowagain - Bill Fox

10. Adriana Thing - Tim Chaplin

**In The Wars download album on timchaplin.bandcamp.com and digital 2022**

1. The Last Thing

2. The Answer In Your Eyes

3. She Said

4. Gonna Get To You

5. Cotton Wool

6. On Your Own

7. Fade Away

8. Let's All Make Friends

9. Same Bus Home

10. The Stars Fell On Sally Brown

11. Lost Cause

12. Watercolour Lane

13. Hazel Eyes

14. Pretty

15. Damage

16. Rag Tag Girl

17. 666

**Sank You download album on timchaplin.bandcamp.com and digital 2022**

1. Penny For Jekyll

2. Lioness

3. Spill

4. Boxing Duke

5. Speed Dive

6. Spots

7. Scuffs

8. Mismotiv8

9. Catching Fire

10. As Above And So Below

11. Haiku

12. Killing Floor

13. Slow Vinyl

14. Put It On Me

15. Molecules

16. Hummingbirds

17. Magnetically Excited

18. Albany's Law

19. What Happiness Wants

**Your Fireworks Or Mine? download album on timchaplin.bandcamp.com and digital 2022**

1. Brown Hair

2. Nothing, I Suppose

3. Deep In The Darks

4. Your Heart And My Mind Will Stay

5. Stuck In A Movie

6. Strange Glue

7. New Clover

8. Since You Went Away

9. Little Doll

10. Beautiful Daisy

11. Lie Lie Lie

12. In The Darks

13. Found Myself

14. Someone Else's House

15. Happy w/

16. Hours And Hours

17. Darks

18. Best Little Timeslip Lately

**Screaming Blue Murder download album on timchaplin.bandcamp.com and digital 2023**

1. Wavy Lines

2. Only An Angel

3. Love Is Like

4. Sandcastles

5. Festival On Me

6. Outta The Blue

7. Maybe It Was Your Mother

8. The Process Of Lying / Crying

9. Hollywood Serene

10. Now It's Only Noise

11. Judy, Jackie-Wise

12. Certified Maybe

13. If You Wanna Stay

14. Nearly You

15. Everywhere And Nowhere Baby

16. You Know Where I Live

**Put You In A Song download EP on timchaplin.bandcamp.com and digital 2023**

1. Put You In A Song

2. Message To Send

3. Nobody Else Here

4. Bad News

5. Nearly You (Electric)

**Time To Go download EP on timchaplin.bandcamp.com and digital 2023**

1. Time To Go

2. Nobody That You Know

3. Miss And Master Mentally

4. Cobwebs

5. Sing Sad Softly

**Use Our Angels download EP on timchaplin.bandcamp.com and digital 2023**

1. Use Our Angels

2. And You Will And I Will

3. Nothing To Defend

4. No Regrets

5. Où Est Suzy Blue?

**Friends download EP on timchaplin.bandcamp.com and digital 2023**

1. Friends

2. Weird Kissy Thing

3. Dead End

4. Undressing To Kill

5. Nearly You (Jewellery Box)

**Plague Of Rocks download album on timchaplin.bandcamp.com and digital 2023**

1. People Take Pictures

2. Bad Inside

3. Don't Share

4. Pain Pills & Ache Pills

5. I'm Not

6. Green About It

7. Marilyn Monroe Repeating

8. Cornflower Blue Days

9. Paint It Green

10. Numbers Of Three

11. Took You

12. You Take

**Thinking In English download album on timchaplin.bandcamp.com and digital 2023**

1. L Is For You

2. Never Saw

3. Petal Pushing

4. About Your Head

5. Coco Thin

6. Make Me

7. Unlucky As

8. Girl Called Crying

9. Two New Shoes

10. Scattershot

11. Mind A Man

12. Like Mine

13. Lies On

14. Gimme Bones

15. About This Girl

# Don't miss out!

Visit the website below and you can sign up to receive emails whenever Tim Chaplin publishes a new book. There's no charge and no obligation.

https://books2read.com/r/B-A-JRMBB-LEDXC

BOOKS2READ

Connecting independent readers to independent writers.

# Also by Tim Chaplin

A Mile Away In The Blink Of An Eye
The Stories In Front Of The Songs

Watch for more at https://timchaplin.bandcamp.com.

## About the Author

Tim Chaplin is a musician, songwriter, producer, composer, artist and writer.

Read more at https://timchaplin.bandcamp.com.